Honey the Rock Hound

Honey the Rock Hound

A Puppy Dies a Family Mourns

Thomas Anonymous

Copyright © 2019 by Thomas Anonymous.

ISBN   Softcover   978-1-951469-89-4

All rights reserved. No part of this book may be reproduced or transmitted in any form or by any means, electronic or mechanical, including photocopying, recording, or by any information storage and retrieval system without express written permission from the author, except in the case of brief quotations embodied in critical reviews and certain other non-commercial uses permitted by copyright law.

Printed in the United States of America.

To order additional copies of this book, contact:
Bookwhip
1-855-339-3589
www.bookwhip.com

Introduction

There was never a lack of things for ten year old Joey to do in his little Maine town. There was church school, cub scouting, trout fishing in nearby streams, a wonderful children's library at the college and a first class outdoor recreation facility.

Someone was always taking him for a boat ride, water skiing or fishing on the sparkling pond nearby. On Saturday evenings when the weather was nice, nearly everyone for miles around turned out to watch stock-car racing at the local speedway.

Often, on winter evenings, parents would bring marshmallows and supervise a huge bonfire on the frozen bog off the main street. Whole families would come out for skating parties. Cross country ski trails at the college were popular for young and old alike..

Ice shacks and fishing holes dotted the pond in the winter. The state saw to it that there were plenty of brown trout for sportsmen, and a few extra for eagles that swooped down and made off with them as soon as fishermen got them off their hooks.

Each winter the snowmobile club sponsored a giant chicken barbeque to benefit a camp for children with disabilities. It seemed like it was always on the coldest day of the year.

Many young people competed in area horse shows. Joey often went with friends to help. Sometimes his friend Debbie let him ride her gentle Appaloosa, Babe around the field.

Each year, Joey looked forward to the day his dad took him to the agricultural fair. Food, handcrafts and home made items were in abundance. Joey was fascinated by demonstrations of border collies that herded sheep by silent commands. He never imagined how smart dogs could be. Yes, there was <u>everything</u> a ten year old boy could want to do in his small Maine town except....

Surprise

One morning Joey's dad said, "Get changed up. We've got a surprise for you." A few minutes later, the family was traveling over Fox Ridge, by Joey's school, heading south along the beautiful Maine coast. His mom had a popular swap-and-sell-it guide open on her lap. Pretty soon she told Joey's dad to slow down. "Take your next right, up the hill… that's the place."

A middle aged lady answered the door and smiled. "I'm Mrs. Gorman," she said. After everyone was introduced, she said to them, "come right in, this way,…. they're out here."

Joey wasn't sure what was going on, but he followed his folks into the house, through the kitchen, dining room, living room…. and there, in the corner of the sun porch, in a large wicker basket, were five of the tiniest Cocker Spaniel puppies Joey had ever seen, all cuddled up to their mother on a warm blanket.

"Oh, Mom,…Dad,… Aren't they **CUTE**", Joey exclaimed!

"It's OK to pick them up," Mrs. Gorman said. They're all weaned, and their mother is just a sweetie. She won't bite you. "It's all right dear," his mother said. "Would you like one of them?" Joey wanted to laugh and cry at the same time. It was almost too good to believe. "Ohhh, yes," he said, as he got down on his knees.

Time stood still for everyone. He picked each pup up and cuddled it in his arms. Finally he turned to his folks, "I know just which one I want, if it's all right." "Which one's that?" said his dad. "The little honey colored one with the curly ears," Joey replied. Joey's dad picked the pup up, held it close to his face and looked into the little dog's eyes. He spoke softly to it. and the puppy wagged it's tail. Joey's mom reached up and patted it on the head. "That's a great choice," his dad said. "Nice dog!" A few moments later Joey looked, and his Dad had the pup standing up in the palm of his hand.

"Is it a little boy dog or a girl?" Joey asked Mrs. Gorman. "It's a little girl dog," she replied "and she doesn't have a name yet." "Oh, good," exclaimed Joey. "I know what I want to call her." " Can't I even help pick her name?" his mother kiddingly quipped. "Well, Mom," said Joey, she's such a little <u>honey</u>. That's what I want to call her. Her coat's just the color of honey, too!" Please, Mom, is that all right?" "Is that OK by you," she asked Joey's dad? "Yup," he chuckled " I couldn't 'ave picked a better name myself."

Settling In

The next weeks were busy ones at Joey's house. Honey marked every rug in it. Joey kept busy just cleaning up after her. Joey's folks bought a little harness and a leash so Joey could take her for walks. Joey did walk her, often, to every house in the neighborhood. He usually had to carry her home, as she'd hang her head so low her ears dragged on the ground when she was tired.

"Can I take her over in the field in back of McPherson's and let her run?" Joey asked one day. "**Good Lord, NO!**" his Dad exclaimed. "The eagles would have her for lunch."

Will The Real Honey Please Stand Up

One day Joey's mom bumped something hard under the recliner as she was vacuuming. It was a small rock. A little later, when she moved the magazine rack she spotted another one about the same size. Each time she vacuumed, she'd find different rocks placed in such a way that no one would notice them. She decided to watch Honey closely.

Joey had learned that Honey would chase anything that was thrown for her – toys, tennis balls, sticks, anything. She particularly liked to chase rocks. Each time Joey threw one into the woods, Honey would hop up and down like a bunny, trying to see where it would end up. She'd paw around in the underbrush for long periods of time, half yipping, half growling until she found the very same rock that had been thrown. No matter how tired she'd get, she'd want to keep going.

After Joey got tired of throwing the rock, Honey would take it over near the barn and carefully place it in an out of the way spot. Every time Joey came outdoors, Honey would run over to that spot, pick the rock up in her mouth and toss it at Joey's feet for him to throw for her. Joey would unhitch her and the two of them would play by the hour.

The dog always knew when someone was coming to let her in the house. She'd quickly scurry over to where the rocks were, pick one up and hide it in her mouth. Then she'd trot over so that person could unsnap her harness.

As soon as Honey walked into the kitchen she'd head for another room. One day Joey's mother quietly followed her. Honey weaved in and out around the furniture until she found just the right hiding place. Quietly she dropped the rock on the floor and nudged it under the edge of the furniture with her nose. Joey's mom didn't say anything, but she wondered. "Just why would that dog bring rocks into the house and hide them? If I wait long enough, maybe I can find out.

> Honey's usually close by.
> She's always under the kitchen table when it's meal time,
> hoping someone will slip her a tasty bite to eat.
> During the evening, when anyone is watching TV,
> or the family is together, Honey lays on her tummy
> close by, watching everything that goes on."

One evening, about half way through the dishes, Joey's mom dried her hands and quietly walked to the living room door. To her surprise, there was Honey, stretched out on her back, waving her feet in the air, rolling back and forth against one of the rocks, scratching her back.

Just then Honey spotted her standing there. Quick as a wink, she rolled over onto her feet and gave the rock a quick shove under a chair with her nose. Turning around, she wagged her tail, and came over to Joey's mom to be patted.

Joey's mom laughed right out loud. "The truth's out," she said. "You're not a Cocker Spaniel, you're a **Rock Hound**!" Honey just wagged her tail and rubbed lovingly against her leg.

A Fish Story

One Sunday afternoon, Joey's dad glanced at his watch. "Get Honey's leash," he said. "They're having a Bass Tournament at the beach today. We'll walk down and see them release the fish."

Joey loved the walk to the beach. The road went straight through the cemetery and wound through a wooded area bordering a huge bog. Someone told Joey that years ago a businessmen's sports club bought the bog, making it the first private bird sanctuary in the nation.

Joey's dad pointed out *an* eagle's nest hidden among tall pine trees beside the road. That day an eagle chick the size of a large crow squawked several times when it heard them approaching. Joey's dad explained that it hadn't learned to fly yet and it was hungry.

Dozens of red winged blackbirds were flitting from cat tail to cat tail in the swamp.

"Look at the size of those moose tracks," exclaimed Joey's dad. "What a whopper he must be!".

As they walked along they could look out and see the large stream on the far side of the bog. Several families of Canadian geese and ducks were swimming close to the shoreline for safety. Joey spotted a large crane standing on one leg hidden in a clump of weeds. Only after it made a "glunnk, glunnk" sound did his dad see it.

Joey's dad pointed out where beaver had chewed down large trees trying to build a dam in a stagnant pond beside the road.

"Look," Joey said, as they approached the beach. "those boats look just alike."

"They're bass boats," said his dad. "These guys belong to a club that travels all around this part of the country fishing together." Joey picked Honey up in his arms. A minute later he gently poked his father. "Dad," he said, "their pick-up trucks all look the same too."

The Weighing In

"That large white sign hanging over there has the weight of each fish caught marked on it," Joey's dad said. Joey was watching a man with boots on wading in the water. Another man brought a big plastic bag with a number of bass in it to him. The one in the water opened up the bag, and gently placed it in the water. There was a lot of splashing as fish that were in the bag took off for deep water, all but one. That one rolled over on it's side and feebly moved it's tail up and down. The man quickly grabbed it with both hands and swished it back and forth in the water. "What's he doing?" asked Joey. "He's giving it artificial respiration," his dad said. "That puts more oxygen in it's gills, watch." In a few moments the fish twitched, slapped it's tail on the water, hard, and swam off. Joey cheered. Honey let out a yip, and tried to get down.

Joey's dad said he could remember as a boy there were midget speed boat races right here on this pond. Joey imagined himself racing one and winning a huge trophy. On the way home, Joey's dad said, "You can unhitch Honey's leash. She's big enough now so the eagles can't pick her up."

Honey trotted back and forth in front of them, making an "S" pattern. Each time she went further and further away. Joey and his dad spotted a flock of wild turkeys at the far corner of a cornfield and had forgotten all about Honey. Suddenly, Joey's dad stopped, looked around and cocked his head sideways. Gently he touched Joey on the arm. "Hear that?" he almost whispered. Joey tuned in his hearing. Together they followed the sound. It was Honey. She was stretched out on her back, in a little gulley, rolling from side to side on something. Neither of them could tell what it was. She was certainly enjoying herself rolling on it. The sounds were groans of contentment and bliss.

The two watched quietly for a few moments before Honey spotted them. As soon as did she turned her head and looked away as though she hadn't seen them, and continued rolling from side to side waving her feet in the air.

"OK dog," Joey's father said disgustedly. Taking care not to touch her back, he hooked the leash to Honey's harness. **"You're** going to get a bath, before **you** go in the house, you **stinkin**' dog!" he chuckled.

And Then It Happened

One hot Saturday afternoon Joey's mom decided to take a walk to the store. His dad was in the driveway washing the car, and Joey was tossing rocks for Honey. It wasn't long before her tongue was purple and hanging down from the side of her mouth. She was panting heavily.

"Take it easy on her, Joey, she's pretty tuckered out right now." Joey's dad said. "That stupid dog will hop 'til she drops!" Honey took a long drink of water from a puddle, found a shady spot and flopped down.

In a few minutes the phone rang. "Dad, some of the guys are playing ball at the park They want me to come down too. Is it OK?" Joey called out. "It's OK for an hour or so," his father replied. Joey grabbed his baseball glove and took off running.

Meanwhile, Back Home

Joey's dad was wiping the last drops of water from his spotless car. He was not aware of his wife's approach on the sidewalk across the road. Honey must have recognized her footsteps, even from several hundred feet away. She lifted her head, took one look and dashed off to greet her.

The first thing Joey's dad heard was the screeching of breaks and tires dragging along the pavement. Joey's mother screamed. Joey's dad watched helplessly from his driveway. **"Honey! Honey!"** he yelled, but she didn't even slow down. The driver hadn't spotted Honey until she was almost beside the truck. It was all over in an instant.

A few feet up the road the truck driver stopped. He got out and tried to help calm Joey's mother. Joey's dad ran over from their home and looked at the crumpled ball of fur and blood lying in the dirt. Then he put his big arms around Joey's mom. Tears streamed down his cheeks, as the two of them stood there.

A neighbor came out with a cardboard box, gently lifted the little dog's crumpled body into it and closed the cover. "Can I take her over to Dr. Bates' (the vet's) for you?" he asked. "No, thanks a lot," Joey's dad said, "I want to do it myself. Please just put the box in front of our barn door."

The truck driver told Joey's parents how sorry he was, gave them his business card and climbed up into the big rig again. Slowly he drove off.

Joey gets word

After the ball game was over, Joey began slowly walking home with some of his friends. A few minutes later they met several girls with tennis rackets, walking toward the field. They were talking intently, and one of the girls was sobbing. They almost didn't notice Joey and his friends until one of the boys said, "what's the matter? What's wrong? You're crying!" "A truck just ran over a dog up near Depot Street," one of the girls replied. "It's awful." Joey's heart sank. He felt like he was going to be sick. "What did the dog look like," he managed to ask. "We didn't see the dog," another girl said. "Someone put it in a box before we got there." Joey started to run. "Please God," he prayed. "PLEASE GOD, don't let it be Honey!" All the way home he kept whispering. "Please God, please God, PLEASE!"

Reality

One glance at his folks is all it took for Joey to realize his worst fears. With full force he threw himself against his mother and burst into tears.

"Tell me it ain't true, Mom. Tell me it ain't true!" For a long time he cried and cried. It was as if the tears wouldn't stop. His mother stroked his hair, and gently rubbed his back.

When the family returned home many of the neighbors gathered in their kitchen. Joey's dad explained exactly what had happened. His mother added how she felt when she realized Honey was racing straight towards the truck. It helped Joey to know every last detail.

Joey's buddies followed him into the kitchen. Each of them got around to giving Joey a hug. With each hug tears welled up in Joey's eyes. He really didn't want a pity party right now, but this was different. This was **real**! He **wanted** those hugs.

Tough Questions

"Did Honey really die, or did she just go to sleep?" Joey's friend Tommy wanted to know. "Is she going to wake up again?" "Sometimes people say a person or pet has fallen asleep, when they should say they've died," Joey's mom said. "The expression 'gone to sleep' can be something like when they say, 'crying your eyes out,' or 'laughing your head off.' Honey's really dead. And, Tommy, you don't have to worry. Healthy people don't die if they go to sleep."

"Is Honey going to come back as something else, like a horse, or a bird?" Tommy asked. "No," said Joey's mom. "It's not God's plan. The Bible says that when we die our bodies return to dust and the spirit part of us returns to God. (Ecclesiastics 12:7) Some people think children turn into angels when they die. That's not true either."

Just then, a neighbor came to the door. "I'd just put these in the oven when all the excitement happened," she said. "Would anyone like a chocolate chip cookie?"

Where is She?

Joey asked what happened to Honey's body, and his dad explained that it was in the garage in the paste board box. "Remember Honey just as she was the last time you saw her," his dad said.

Joey stood up straight, took a deep breath, staggered over to another chair, and sat down hard. He was turning pale. Joey's mom grabbed a towel and quickly wet it with cold water. Hurrying over to Joey, she gently washed his face and curled the towel around the back of his neck. For a long time everyone was quiet.

"You know what….. Mom….Dad…" Joey finally said. "What is it dear?" replied his mother. "I… I… I forgot to hook Honey's rope on her when I went down to the ball field." he almost whispered. "If I had 'uv…if I did".. and he began to cry again. "Oooh, it's my fault Honey's dead. If only,…if only….."

Joey's dad walked over and picked him up in his strong arms. He sat down in the chair and pulled Joey across his lap. "You know, Joey," he said, "I was right here with

Honey, too, and I didn't notice she didn't have her leash on, either. It's partly my fault. We all forget things sometimes," he added. "It just happened. She could have run out in the road any other time that we didn't have her hitched. She hadn't learned how dangerous the road is."

What's Next

Joey's mom had mixed some ice in a pitcher of fruit punch and poured some for Joey. Then she gave some to each of the others. Joey began to feel a little better. "What are you going to do with Honey's body now?" Joey wanted to know. "Well, your mom's got something to say about this," his dad explained, "but I think we have three choices. We can take her body over to Dr. Bates, the vet and he'll have her body cremated. That's one choice. We can take her body out in the woods, and bury it deep, so no animals can get it, or, if mom says it's OK, we can have a little grave for her out back of the house."

Joey's mom started to say, "I wouldn't mind if she's..." but just then Joey broke in. "What's '**cremated**'?" he demanded. "You didn't let your mother finish what she was saying," Joey's dad scolded. "I'm sorry," said Joey, hanging his head. "I don't know what you're talking about. I don't know what Dr. Bates would do." he mumbled.

"I should have explained it better," Joey's dad said. "If Honey's body were to be cremated, it would be taken to a cemetery. and placed in something like a big oven in a gas stove. All that would be left is a few little pieces of her bones, that they call 'cremains'."

"Some people who die are cremated, too. Afterward the families of these people take the 'cremains' and bury them in a family lot at a cemetery, or to a special building where they can go visit. Anyway," he continued, "your mother wanted to say something." "Yes," she continued "I was going to say that I'd like to have her buried out back near my lilac bush." "It's been a long afternoon," said Joey's dad. "We'll go out after supper and decide on just the right place for her grave." Later that evening, after everyone had agreed where to bury Honey's body, Joey became very moody. "Mom, Dad," he said. "I'm going out in the barn for a little while. I just want to be with Honey one more time. There's some 'stuff' I want to say to her too, that I didn't get a chance to say before."

"Thanks for telling us where you're going," Joey's dad said. "We would have worried if you hadn't." It was long past bedtime when Joey came in the house. He turned off his light and crawled into bed.

A Brand New Day

Joey was up before breakfast. He sat by the window that looked out on the life-sized bronze animals in the little park across the street. It just didn't seem right not having Honey to take out and put on her leash. He missed the funny little dance and sneeze she did every day for each person as they greeted her. After breakfast Joey's mom asked, "Is your bed made, Joey?" "No!" he snapped. "Why not, dear?" she asked. "I just don't feel like doing it!" Joey growled. He quickly got up from his chair and went out on the back porch, slamming the screen door behind him.

Pretty soon his dad came out with his boots on. "Grab the old ax out of the barn, Joey," he said. "I could use some help with Honey's grave." "I'll be out in a few minutes," Joey replied. Under his breath he muttered, "when I get around to it." His dad gently picked up the box with Honey's crumpled little body in it and carried it out back. Joey just sat on the porch and let the morning sun warm him. Joey's dad came around the corner of the barn in a little while, took one look at Joey snoozing, and went back to work.

"**Joey**,"... the sound jolted him awake. "Uuuhhhh," he groaned. For a few seconds he didn't know where he was, or who had spoken to him. "Joey," the voice spoke again, this time softer. Now he knew just where it was coming from, and exactly whose it was. "What!" he snapped. It was Lyndsay, a classmate from up the street. "We were away yesterday," she said. "Tell me about Honey." Joey took a long look at Lyndsay. He didn't particularly like girls and of all the girls he knew, he liked her the least of all.

"I'm busy," he said," I got a lot a stuff I hafta do," and he quickly got up and started into the house. The screen door hadn't even closed behind him when he bumped smack into his mother. "Oooops," he said, and stopped.

"**Joey**," his mother scolded. She bent over him, a few inches from his face and looked him straight in the eye. "You get yourself right out there and tell Lyndsay you're sorry for the way you talked to her! That little girl came down here to ask you about Honey. If you don't want to talk about it right now, you ask her to come back again, and you be nice when you talk to her too. Now, **march**!"

Lyndsay was just riding her bike out of the driveway when Joey walked out on the porch. "Lyndsay," he called, "please come back a minute." Lyndsay wheeled her bike around, drove up close to the porch. Leaning on the handle bars, she said. "Wha'da'ya want." "Uuuhhh," Joey began. "I... I.. I'm sorry I wasn't nice to you," he said. "I don't want to talk about Honey right now," he continued, and started into the house again.

"Lyndsay," Joey's mother said. She had come out on the porch and was standing there. "If you want to stop a minute, I'll tell you about what happened yesterday. Oh, by the way, there's still a couple of chocolate chip cookies that Mrs. Roy brought over yesterday. I'll get 'em for us if you want me to and some cold milk too. Joey can go do whatever it was he had to do, and we'll sit here on the porch and talk about Honey."

"My mom really knows how to make a tough point," Joey thought to himself. He went in and sat on his bed for a long time. Then he got up and slowly pulled the sheets and blanket up around the pillow. A few minutes later he dragged himself out to the garage, looking for the old ax. It wasn't there so he walked out back to where his dad was digging. There was the ax, covered with dirt, where his dad had cut some roots of the lilac bush. "I'm ready to help you now." he said.

Joey was surprised just how deep his dad had dug Honey's grave. It was almost done, but Joey's father had him dig it a little deeper. "There, that's enough," he said finally. "No animal's going to dig that deep. Go ask your mother if she'll come out for a minute." OK said Joey. A few minutes later he followed his mother out back. He'd noticed his dad had made a wooden box to replace the cardboard one and it was already in the grave when he and his mother arrived.

A Moment of Thanks

I thought you might want to say a little prayer before we cover Honey's grave, " Joey's father said. His mother nodded. "That would be nice."

Joey took off his cap, and every one bowed their head. Joey's mother prayed.

> "Dear Heavenly Father, You give life to all things.
> We thank You for giving Honey to us, even for
> such a little while. Thank You that she brought
> so much joy into our lives. We place her little body
> here with the lilacs and flowers, where it will
> return to dust. However we know her spirit is safe
> with you even now. Thank You that we'll all be together with
> you again, someday. We ask that You
> continue to watch over us, and those that we love.
> In Jesus' Name…Amen."

Joey looked up just in time to see his father stuff his handkerchief in his hip pocket. His mother gently dabbed her eyes with her apron. Joey wiped his nose on his sleeve. (If his mother saw him do it, she didn't say anything.) "Joey," his dad said. "If we're going to get this done by lunch time you're going to have to help me. There's a small shovel behind the door in the barn. "Yup," said Joey, as he took off running. "I'll be right with you."

A Space Suit?

By lunchtime Joey was hungry. When he finished eating he sat back in his chair and said, "I don't understand something. How can Honey be in the grave out behind the house, and be with God at the same time?"

"That's a tough one to get your mind around, Joey," his mother said. " You see, it's like this." Do you remember when we saw the astronauts on TV working outside on their space ship in their space suits?" "Sure I do," said Joey. "The space suit didn't do anything unless the astronaut made it happen, right? We're all spirit beings living in space suits,... I guess earth suits would be a better way of saying it. We call our earth suits our bodies. Our bodies can't do anything unless our spirits tell then to. The Bible says that apart from our spirits our bodies are lifeless.**(James 2:26)** (It also says that as surely as there is a physical body there is a spiritual body too. **(I Corinthians 15:44)** This is true for us. I have no reason to believe it's different for animals.

Honey's body couldn't do anything unless Honey's spirit made it happen. Do you understand what I mean?"

"Never thought of it that way before," Joey said. "So when Honey got killed,....run over," Joey stammered, "Where did her spirit go?" "To be with God," his Mom said gently, "our spirits never die. Honey's didn't either." "Will we see Honey again in Heaven?" asked Joey. "I like to think that puppies who have died make kids that are in Heaven happy, just like they do here." his mom replied. "That's one thing the Bible doesn't make clear to me.

We do know that God loves every creature that he has created, and knows when they die.

(Matthew 10:28 – 30
  Psalm 49:12 – 15
  Ecclesiastes 3:19 – 21
  Ecclesiastes 12:7)

How Can That Be

"How come my Sunday School teacher says everybody's not going to go to heaven, and you say all the animals do go there." Joey wanted to know. Joey's dad took a deep breath. "Joey," he said after a long pause. "You play on a baseball team, don't you?" Joey nodded. "Can you play on two teams at the same time?" Joey pondered a long moment. "no way!" he exclaimed. His father continued. "How would your coach or teammates like it if you did?" Joey felt uneasy.

"As Christians, your mother and I believe that if we want to go to heaven, when we die, we've got to play on God's team while we're here on earth. Jesus is the 'coach', and the Bible tells us how to live! God hasn't given animals the knowledge or ability to choose the difference between good and evil," he continued. "Their spirits **all** go back to God when their bodies die. But He has given **you** that knowledge, and He wants you to love Him and trust Him. So, go think about that for a while. We'll talk about it again any time you want to."

"I'm <u>really</u> mad at God!" Joey muttered. "I prayed that it wouldn't be Honey that got run over and it was!" Joey started crying. Joey's mother waited a minute and gave him a hug. "You know," she said, "It's OK to be mad at God. He knows just how you're feeling…**all the time** and He understands. He heard your prayer about Honey, **before** you even prayed it, (**Psalm139**) The truth is, God knows best, He just wants us to love Him and trust Him. Remember, He was right there watching when they killed His Son, and He let them do it. Another thing, no matter how we feel, God doesn't want us to be unkind or hateful to other people." Joey pondered his mother's words for a long time. Finally he said, "OK, Mom. I think I got it. I love you".

What About A New Puppy?

"Mom, Billy's folks said we should get another puppy," Joey said one morning a few days later. "He says they've got all kinds of 'em at the animal shelter in Belfast. All we'd have to do is get it shots and stuff." "Mmm," mused his mom. "We'll sit down later and talk about it. Right now I'm busy."

Joey spent all afternoon daydreaming about a new puppy. "I really do need another puppy, BAD," he thought. "Look at all the stuff I could do with one that I didn't get to do with Honey! I'll bet I could even teach a new one to pick up my toys and play ball with me. What kind will I get this time? What color would it be? What would I name it? S'pose my folks would let me get a border collie?"

After supper, Joey's mom and dad did the dishes. They seemed to be talking seriously between themselves. Joey did his homework, and started to read a book. Pretty soon his mom said, "Let's sit down and talk about Billy's folks' suggestion that we get another puppy." Joey thought, "Oh, wow, it's really goin' to happen! I'm gonna ask for a border collie," and he plunked himself down in a dining room chair.

Joey's dad started out by saying, "You really miss Honey a lot, don't you, son?" Joey started to get teary eyed. He managed to squeak out a weak "yes." "Do you really think a new puppy right now would help very much?" his dad asked. Joey had to fight back the tears. "Well," he said, "I wouldn't have to think about Honey as much as I do."

Joey's mother said something that made him sit up straight." Perhaps we need to think about Honey a little <u>more</u>, before we just forget her and worry about a new puppy. All those thoughts and feelings we have about her have to be dealt with sometime. If we don't deal with them now we'll have to deal with them later on when it could be much more difficult, and even cause serious problems," she said. "What kinds of thoughts and feelings are you talking about, Mom?" asked Joey. "Well, one of them might be the way you were hateful to Lyndsay when she came over the other day. Do you remember that?" Joey hung his head. "If you don't deal with your feelings of anger because Honey died you might be mean to a puppy," she explained. "that wouldn't be good, either, would it?"

"And, another thing," his Mother continued, "might be when you said "If only I'd put Honey's leash on her before I went down to the ball field that day. You felt guilty that you hadn't done more to keep the accident from happening, right?" Joey just sniffled. "You need time to forgive yourself for that. Those are the kinds of thoughts and feelings I was talking about. They're all perfectly normal, and everyone that has someone or some thing they love that has died has to work through them.

"Don't forget, Joey, you can always go to God, and ask Him for forgiveness. Sometimes it feels like we're in a cage or prison until we do go to Him. He's **always** ready to forgive us when we ask Him to, you know!"

I heard you telling your friend Tommy that sometimes you make believe the accident really didn't happen and play like you would if Honey was right there with you. You said you even talk just as if she were there, too. Do you remember doing those things?" his mother went on. Joey nodded his head. "I'm sure you do, If we make believe that Honey didn't really die, that isn't being truthful is it? Making believe the accident didn't really happen doesn't make it go away, either, does it?" Joey started to cry.

Sometimes We're In A World Of Our Own

"You know what, Joey," his dad said. "There were two or three things we asked you to do right after Honey was killed. Some of the time I don't think you even heard a word we said. You were like a little zombie." Joey blew his nose. "But it's **OK**, his dad went on. Most people are like that, at first, when something bad jerks the rug out from under them. Sometimes we're like a turtle that pulls his head inside it's shell and hopes the bad stuff goes away. We need lots of time to come out of our shells and admit the bad stuff really happened."

"It helps a lot to be able to talk with other people about it too. We should always turn to God and ask Him to help us no matter what. If we have to start worrying about a new puppy and 'stuff' all the feelings we have about Honey, the bad stuff will just keep rolling around inside us. It can make us sick. Can you understand what I'm trying to tell you, son?" "I think so," Joey said. "OK," said his dad. "We'll talk about it some more any time you want to."

An Art Project

"Right now I want you to get out your new markers and a big piece of paper, and draw a picture for me," Joey's dad said. "I want it to be something you remember doing with Honey. If you want to work on it three or four days that's OK. When it's done, we'll put it up on the refrigerator for a while. If you want me to, I'll buy you a picture frame so you can hang it in your room."

"I just thought about something," said his mom. "We'll collect all the pictures we've taken of Honey, even way back when she was a puppy. My friend Sue teaches scrapbook decorating. We'll make a nice memorial scrapbook of Honey's 'stuff' and I'll ask Sue to help us decorate it, OK?" "That'll be neat," exclaimed Joey, "I've got a few saved upstairs in my bureau drawer."

"Oh", said his mom. "There's something I forgot to tell you. Sunday afternoon we're going to have everyone in the neighborhood here to remember Honey. Uncle Tim's going to bring some of his homemade ice cream. Remember, he and Aunt Tonya took care of Honey while we were in Florida, and they want to be with us too." "Cool," said Joey.

Getting Ready For Sunday

Joey's mom kept him busy Saturday. He helped dust and vacuum. He even found another rock Honey had hidden under a chair.

The scrapbook his mother bought was beautiful. "We've got to leave plenty of space between the pictures for decorations," she explained. "My friend Sue is coming later to show us ways to make the pages really nice."

"We've got the whole coffee table to use for things that'll help everyone remember Honey as they knew her," Joey's mom said. "What do you think we should put on it?" "Well, we ought'a put some of Honey's rocks there," Joey said. after a little thought. "The rocks are a <u>great</u> <u>idea</u>," his mother confirmed. "And, we'll put the scrapbook on the dining room table opened up. I know what," she continued. "I'll get her brush. I spent a lot of time brushing burdocks out of those curly ears of hers. That brush'll be a good reminder." "I'm going to put her leash on the coffee table too," Joey said. It'll help everyone remember all the fun I had taking her on walks."

Just then Joey's dad came in. "Did anyone think about a little guest book for everyone to sign?" he asked. That would be really neat," Joey exclaimed. "I've got to go out and get a few things for tomorrow," Joey's mother said. "Why don't you come with me Joey, and we'll pick one up at the drug store."

Sunday Was Bright And Sunny

Joey and his folks hurried home from church and quickly tidied up the house. Joey's mom was sweeping off the steps when a big blue car drove in the driveway.. It was Aunt Tonya and Uncle Tim. "I'm glad you got here safely," Joey's dad said. "You're just in time for lunch."

Uncle Tim opened the car door for Aunt Tonya, and lifted out a big vase of fresh flowers. "I hope these cheer everyone up a bit," he said. "We just picked them up at Stacie's flower shop on the way by." "Oooh, they're <u>lovely</u>," Joey's mom exclaimed! "Let's put them in the middle of the coffee table with Honey's other things."

Aunt Tonya gave Joey a colored picture of Honey when she was still tiny. Joey's eyes watered up. Aunt Tonya gave him a hug. "This'll look nice right beside the flowers." she said as she placed it on the coffee table. "We took that picture while Honey was staying with us during your Florida trip."

Soon the neighbors began arriving. Joey's mother had soft music playing on the stereo. Mrs. Roy brought a big dish of her chocolate chip cookies. Several people began looking at the newly decorated scrapbook. Many of Joey's friends came, even Lyndsay from up the street. Joey took a quick look at her. Then he stopped and took a second look. Suddenly, he realized, "She's pretty, all dressed up."

Everyone sat down in the living room. Joey and his friends sat on the floor near the coffee table. Lyndsay sat in a chair. Joey's mother began. "I want to be sure each of you sign our guest book today. Some of you haven't met my sister Tonya and her husband Tim. Please introduce yourselves. We can thank them for the home made ice cream. Be sure and look at the scrapbook on the dining room table with pictures of Honey," she continued. "My friend Sue, over there on the couch, helped us decorate it."

Aunt Tonya and Uncle Tim told everyone about taking care of Honey while Joey and his folks were in Florida. They said they grew so fond of her that they didn't want to let her go home. Joey's mom told about the way Honey acted when they went to get her after the trip. She said, "Honey wouldn't even look at us, when we got there. She put her head down, and just turned around and walked into the other room without even wagging her tail. I'm not sure if she was mad because we left her, or if she didn't want to come home." Everyone laughed. "It wasn't funny at the time," she said. "She wouldn't have anything to do with any of us for **over a week.**" Joey's dad talked about the wooly old slipper on the coffee table. "Honey used to try and drag it to bed with her every night when she was a pup." he said. She'd lay on the wooly part of it, on her belly, and chew on the toe."

One of Joey's friends brought an old tennis ball that Honey had chewed a hole in. Another boy's mother brought a squeak toy Honey liked to play with at their house. She said Honey would bring the toy and squeak it until she threw it. Then she'd bring it back and do the same thing over and over again. "I had to hide the toy before she'd quit!"

Another neighbor remembered the time Honey crawled in behind some old stuff in their garage. "When she came out she was so covered with dust we thought her name should be changed to Dusty."

A neighbor Mrs. Viceroy said, "I took a video of Honey chasing rocks when she was over here one day. Would anyone like to see it now?" Everyone said they would. She replayed it several times and each time everyone laughed to see Honey hopping like a bunny, as she tried to see where the rocks landed in the woods. Each time she hopped, her ears flapped straight out like wings.

After a-while everyone finished talking about things they remembered. They all agreed that **Honey The Rock Hound** was a special "one of a kind" dog. Joey's dad opened a small box with a bronze grave marker that just said "Honey" on it. "Would anyone like to walk out back with me while I put this on Honey's grave?" he asked. Everyone nodded yes. Joey and his friends got up and led the way. Joey's mom bent down and picked up the vase of flowers from the coffee table as she went by.

After Joey's dad finished securing the marker his mother set the vase on it. Joey took one of Honey's rocks out of his pocket and placed it in front of the vase.

Aunt Tonya said, "If it's all right, I'd like to read my favorite poem. I've loved it ever since I was a little girl." Joey's dad nodded approval. Everybody came in a little closer around Honey's grave. Carefully she unfolded a piece of paper from her purse and began. "It's by Elizabeth Gardner Reynolds. and it's called…

I Wonder If Christ Had A Little Black Dog

> I wonder if Christ had a little black dog
> All curly and wooly like mine
> With two silky ears and a nose round and wet
> And eyes brown and tender that shine.
> I'm sure if He had that the little black dog
> Knew right from the start He was God!
> That he needed no proof that Christ was Divine
> But just worshipped the ground where He trod.
> I'm afraid that He didn't, because I have read
> How He prayed in the garden alone,
> When all of His friends and disciples had fled

Even Peter, the one called a "stone".
And oh I am sure that a little black dog
With a heart so tender and warm,
Would never have left Him to suffer alone
But creeping right under His arm, would have licked those dear
fingers in agony clasped
And counting all favors but lost,
When they took Him away would have trotted behind
And followed Him right to the cross."

Joey looked around. There wasn't a dry eye anywhere. "That was beautiful," Joey's mom said. Joey's dad nodded. "Lets go have some of Uncle Tim's homemade ice cream."

Epilogue

Will The Real Honey Please Say Woof?
From the very first time the "real" Honey entered our lives she captured everyone's heart. She had no favorites, nor was anyone jealous when she was lavishing her affections on another.

Each time my wife cleaned house she gathered a pile of small rocks throughout the house where Honey had hidden them, She'd make a pile of them on the radiator by the back door for me to dispose of.

Regardless of where Honey was in the house, she instinctively knew when I was about to discard them and appeared, almost from nowhere, wagging her tail, and begging me to throw them for her to chase.

* * * * *

Honey became completely involved in each project my wife and I ever tackled. If we moved a wheelbarrow load of leaves, for instance, she trotted ahead of us in an "S" pattern to our destination, constantly glancing back to be sure we were following her.

We lived at the busiest intersection in town.

Oil trucks were constantly roaring by on their way to and from the coast. Trucks loaded with grain supplied the faltering poultry industry. Honey <u>never</u> wandered near the road....except **once!**

I was cutting trees on a steep slope behind the house one day. Honey was lying at the top of the knoll watching me. The first tree I cut got caught in another. The second one, with the branches of the first still entwined, tangled up in a third. There was no controlling the direction the trees would fall when I cut the third. Together they went crashing onto the building, taking roofing shingles, boards and siding with them down to the exact spot where Honey had been lying.

My first thought was, "Oh no, I've killed my dog!"

I rushed to the place the trees had fallen, calling at the top of my voice, "Honey! Honey!" Nothing. No sound at all. No whimpering, no yelps of pain. Just deafening silence.

I took off running to the front of the house thinking, "maybe, just maybe, she had gotten up and gone out there without my seeing her." No Honey. I dashed back, and began frantically moving branches to look more closely. Still nothing. At last I gave up, and slowly walked back around the building. My head was down, my hands were in my pockets and I was almost crying.

"Are you looking for Honey, Tom?" a familiar voice spoke to me. I swallowed hard. A car had pulled over to the curb, and a friend had rolled the window down.

"How'd **you** know?" I asked. "She's way over across the road at that house out back", she said. "They have a new dog". A couple minutes later I looked and Honey was slowly trotting across the road toward home ignoring me, and pretending I didn't see her. I was so mad at her I wanted to kill her and so happy she was alive I wanted to hug her!

* * * * *

I never realized that a dog had emotions until we returned from a trip to Florida with our daughter. We had left Honey with my wife's sister and husband. When we returned she completely snubbed us all for about a week.

* * * * *

Honey The Protector

One evening my wife and I were home alone with Honey. Two men came to the door, and almost pushed their way in when I opened it. They walked into the den demanding some gasoline. Luckily, I had a small amount in the garage. Honey went with me, placing herself between me and the men, even as I poured. God only knows what might have happened had she not been there and gone with me.

* * * * *

The hero of our story, Joey was named for my grandson, who, as a little boy continually threw rocks for Honey until I thought she was going to die! She just wouldn't quit chasing them and Joey just kept on heaving them as hard as he could into the bushes. Each time, Honey would drag herself back with the same rock in her mouth, panting badly.

* * * * *

We did not live in A "One Horse Town!"

It seemed like every kid in town including my daughter had a horse. There was a riding club and frequent horse shows in the area. Anyone had to have overshoes or boots on to walk down main street. Come to think of it, there were times when you couldn't **walk** down main street!

Honey The Rock Hound

* * * * *

There was one time when Honey's passion for chasing rocks (or anything else) got her in trouble. One day she watched someone casting a wooden fishing lure (often referred to as a "plug") from a dock at camp. It was about the size of a large man's thumb with two sets of hooks hanging down from the underside of it. Each time the fisherman swung the pole over his shoulder to cast, the dangling plug would swing from side to side, two or three feet above the dock.

Honey had it all figured out. One time, when the plug came back over the fisherman's shoulder, Honey made a lunge for it. Fortunately she miscalculated. The plug was faster than she was. Instead of catching it in her mouth, one hook imbedded itself in her ear. Frantically she tried to dislodge it but the other hooks got tangled in the back of her leg.. What a pathetic sight! She was curled up in a ball completely helpless. As soon as I could, I got to her, and picked her up. Without a whimper she just relaxed, stopped struggling, and allowed us to cut the hooks loose.

One morning on a walk near the pond, a baby skunk came out in the road and hopped toward us wanting to play. I knew mamma was somewhere close by, so I turned and ran. Thankfully Honey did too.

The story of Honey The Rock Hound is really about the lives of two very special dogs. The real Honey had to be put down. She could no longer control her bladder. Her predecessor, "Dusty", a spaniel - beagle mix bolted in front of a car on her way to greet my wife and daughter. Friends took care of her crumpled little body for me.

We had named her Dusty because as soon as she arrived at our home she immediately found the dustiest place in the house behind a radiator, and came out looking like a dust mop.

* * * * *

The grieving process is similar, regardless of whether it's for a pet, or a parent or anyone else we love. The emotional grip grief has over our lives is powerful. Feelings of guilt, fear and unforgiveness. "If **only we had** done such and such, our loved one would not have died," or **"If we hadn't done such and such,** things would have been different. **There is nothing we can do to change the past!** We need to let go of it and appreciate the blessing we have right now!

Often a person in grief fears things unnecessarily. Fear of being alone, fear of pain we might experience. Fear of the unknown. Fear that we might not be able to meet others expectations. The truth is, most fears are totally unfounded. Fear keeps us from moving out and being all we could be.

One woman lived in bitterness and anger for over ten years because she refused to forgive a man who, while driving drunk, struck and killed her son on his bicycle. She had seen it happen. She said that when she finally went to his house, and told him she forgave him, she began to heal! The end of that story is, for many years after that this same woman helped many parents whose children had died.

The Lord's Prayer in the Bible says that God will "forgive us our trespasses **as we** forgive those who trespass against us." Strife compounds grief. Only true forgiveness sets us free.

There's another part of forgiveness that keeps us in bondage. That's asking God's forgiveness for whatever things we have done wrong. "Yes", you say, "But you don't know what I did. It's so bad I'm sure God will never forgive me". That's the whole reason for Jesus dying on the cross and rising again so we **could** be forgiven. It's free! All we have to do is ask for it! We can't be good enough, we can't buy it and we can't earn it!

Let go of the guilt, let go of the fear. Forgive, be forgiven and we're free!

No One Is Immune From Grief.

We continually deal with it. Someone we know well has a social event, and we're not invited. A bread winner loses their job. Someone else gets the promotion that we think we should have. Or we've had a crush on someone of the opposite sex and were rejected. There's no "right" or "wrong" way to mourn our losses. We all need family and friends to help us get through them. We need to be careful that no one grieving isolates themselves.

At first we don't want to believe what's happened. We're stunned, in a daze, bewildered, helpless. We have fears, anxiety and sometimes we panic. It's possible that we may have many of these emotions even before a death occurs, if we realize a loved one is going to die.

Almost always there's a period of anger.
Sometimes it comes right after the loved one dies, or it can happen weeks, months, or even years afterward.
Sometimes we're mad at God.
Sometimes we feel that the one who died

cheated us out of pleasure, or other things.
Sometimes we're mad at anybody who just happens to be around at the time – doctors, nurses, funeral service personnel.
Sometimes we'll even say things that are hateful or unkind.

If someone says unkind things we shouldn't take it personally. The person usually realizes their outburst was uncalled for. They cry profusely, (releasing pent up emotions), and apologize.

The powerful emotions we experience when we grieve **are normal.** If a person can't find ways to deal with them in an acceptable way, serious problems can develop. We should be ready to refer them to a doctor or counselor.

Death is a robber! Even though it may be painful, the best way to deal with our feelings is to talk about them. It's like a visit to the dentist. It's painful. It hurts for a while, but long term benefits far outweigh the pain.

Adult children sometimes over-protect elderly parents.

Well-meaning parents of adult children may take over if a grandchild dies. That only delays the normal grieving process and robs the parents of the opportunity to take part in meaningful closure.

Don't take or give anyone medicine unless the doctor prescribes it. Medications usually have the affect of complicating the grieving process. They wear off, and later the one medicated is left alone to deal with the grief.

Take lots of time to sort out long term strategies before selling property, making important decisions, hurrying into other relationships, moving, changing set patterns or routines. Always talk things over with family, friends and/or legal counsel first.

People often isolate themselves following the death of a loved one. Try and get them out of the house. Be specific. Say, "I'll be here Saturday at 9:00AM and we'll go have coffee (or something similar). AARP, hospices, clergy, therapists, hospitals and funeral service personnel can recommend support groups. If there are none available start your own! For help, e-mail pointthewayenterprises@juno.com

As often as possible, have the person talk about the one who has died **by name**. Go over all of the events surrounding the death. Help the person "hear" what **they** are saying by repeating their words back to them. For example, say, "What I hear you saying is—" (Rephrase the words so they're not exactly the same, but have the same meaning.) We can also say the exact same thing back to the person in the form of a question. These two ways of saying the same thing to the grieving person helps get them to "open up."

Helpful Questions To Ask

When did you first become aware of the seriousness of your loved one's illness?

When did they realize how serious it was?

Did you talk with him / her about it?

Did your loved one want to talk about it ?

Was it difficult? Was it important to them? To you?

Did it help them? Did it help you?

What differences did your loved one make in your life?

In the lives of others?

Are there things you wish you could have said to your loved one that you didn't get a chance to say?

Would you want to tell me what they are?

Would it help to write a goodbye letter to your loved one?

Do everything possible to help the person talk about their grief. To get the pent up emotions out. Many people in mental hospitals and prisons haven't resolved their grief.

Don't lie to a child!

> Don't say a pet or loved one has gone on a trip, gone to sleep or is visiting someone. Sooner or later (sometimes years later) the child has to deal with the truth. "If Grammy's on a trip, why is everyone crying?"

We need to be **extra careful** of the language we use with children. If we tell them someone has "gone to sleep" they could be terrified about going to sleep. The same thing goes for telling a child God needed another little angel. God didn't need another angel. Angels are created beings, totally different from humans. God didn't need another little rose for his flower garden either. The child will still be a child when it's spirit goes to be with God. One child rejected it's mother because she "lost" the new baby at the hospital.

It is not uncommon for children to blame themselves for the death of a pet or loved one. The child needs to be reassured that his actions didn't make the pet or

person die, any more than what they said or did had anything to do with keeping them alive.

The attitude we have following the death of a dear one will have a great affect on a child's attitude in later years. We need to spend extra time with a child. Give them plenty of physical affection and understanding. They need reassurance that they'll be taken care of should both parents die. Encourage a child to talk about any fears they may have.

Sometimes a child (or adult) will seem to be grieving way out of proportion to whatever it is that has happened. **Don't squelch the emotions.** Someone may be grieving about **something serious that happened in the past** where they didn't have an opportunity to "let it out." Whatever the situation is, encourage them to talk about it and do meaningful things such as writing their thoughts down, writing a poem, drawing or painting a picture of something they remember doing with the loved one. Listening to the loved one's favorite music sometimes helps. Ask the person to express their thoughts to you, a family member, or if things seem serious to a clergy person or psychotherapist.

Here are some helpful things to ask someone who has lost a pet

How many years was Sabrina part of your family? Did she bond with one member of the family more than with others? Tell me about Fido's personality. She always seemed so good natured to me. Do you remember a time when Woofie did something special? What is your fondest memory of Sedgley? You mentioned that Teddy brought you the paper every morning. I'll bet you're having a tough time adjusting to the change in your routine. You said Rex slept at the foot of your bed every night. You must miss having your feet warmed so well. I think it's sweet Buffy shared your doughnut with you every morning while you were eating breakfast. Or... What I hear you say is, Pete stood at the back door every morning wagging his tail 'til you got ready to take him for his walk. What about the stormy days when you couldn't go for a walk?

Tell me about Tadbury's diabetes? Did her personality change as the disease progressed? When did you realize something wasn't quite right? What do you miss most now that Kobie has died? Did your kids get to say goodbye to Freckles before youi had to have her put down? Did you say the things to her that you wanted to before she died? Is your family getting together to remember Kongo and talk about their memories of him? Want a hand getting things organized when the time comes?

Let the grieving person know you **really** care.

To Help The Grieving Person

Be there for them! Remember, birthdays, holidays and anniversaries are especially tough if anyone is alone following the death of a loved one!

A Divorce, or Separation Can Be Worse Than A Death

When someone dies, family and community come together to love, support and affirm the life of that person. Fortunately, most continue their support long after the death. When there has been a divorce or separation, few people really know how to act, or what to say, so they often say nothing. Worse, they tend to avoid the one grieving. Friends feel awkward around the person. It's possible that one or the other spouse of a friendly couple may feel their marriage threatened by the now single person.

Many of the suggestions regarding helping someone grieving the death of a loved one apply when there's a divorce or separation. The hurting person will almost certainly harbor much anger and resentment toward the one that has left. Help that person express their feelings in an acceptable way. Try and get them to remember some of the **good** qualities about that other person. There had to have been **some** for the person to have had a loving relationship before. **Be there for them.**

Some Ways To Avoid Depression

Visit a shut-in. **Renew** an acquaintance. Volunteer at a hospital, nursing home, soup kitchen, food pantry, senior citizens organization, school etc. **Take someone** to lunch, play, or a show. **Invite** friends for a time of sharing. **Heal** a broken relationship. **Make** a new friend. **Get involved** in a church or club. **Learn** to play a new musical instrument. **Buy** yourself something special. **Bake** some cookies, **give** them away. **Change** your routine. Do for yourself. **Do** only what you really want to do. **Write** down your (holiday) expectations and **prioritize** them. **Share** your memories. **Talk** over old times. The grieving process takes many months or even years.

Don't imagine what you'd do "if things were different." **They're not different.**

Make a success with **whatever it is** you have to work with.

Stop saying, "If I had the time." The only way to **find** the time or **have** the time is to **make the time.**

Try not to worry. Anxiety can become a serious problem

Keep your mind active – read a book.

Don't be disagreeable. Don't criticize.

Forgive. Only in forgiveness will healing begin

May God Bless You

GRIEF RECOVERY RESOURCES

pointthewayeterprisesa@juno.com

* Honey The Rock Hound For Kids

* Grief Recovery & Support Groups

* Grief Recovery In The Marketplace

* Grief Recovery In The Church

* Grief Recovery In The Classroom

* Grief Recovery In The Nursing Home & Hospital

* Grief REccovery For Hospital Chaplaincy Service

* Grief REcovery For Florists

* Grief Reccovery For Hair Dressers & Beauticians

* Grief Recovery For Police, Fire Fighters & Veterans

* Grief Recovery In Prison

* Grief Recovery For Veterinarian Clients

www.ingramcontent.com/pod-product-compliance
Lightning Source LLC
Chambersburg PA
CBHW030132100526
44591CB00009B/624